I0434930

The Big Book of Hard to Remember Information

General Information

For security reasons, in this section you should write reminders of codes and passwords. If you write the actual codes and passwords, then make sure you keep this book in a very safe place.

TV subscription
card number:

Internet connection name:

Internet password:

Computer Passwords:

House Alarm Code:

Location of spare keys:

Important Telephone Numbers

Police:

Doctor:

Hospital:

Dentist:

Others:

Name:

Number:

Name:

Number:

Important Telephone Numbers

Name:

Number:

Name:

Number:

Name:

Number:

Name:

Number:

Name:

Number:

National Insurance Numbers

Name:

Number:

Name:

Number:

Name:

Number:

Name:

Number:

Name:

Number:

National Insurance Numbers

Name:

Number:

Name:

Number:

Name:

Number:

Name:

Number:

Name:

Number:

Passport

Numbers

Name:

Number:

Name:

Number:

Name:

Number:

Name:

Number:

Name:

Number:

Passport Numbers

Name:

Number:

Name:

Number:

Name:

Number:

Name:

Number:

Name:

Number:

House Deeds

Note: You may not have any house deeds as such if you live in an area which has a modern registered land system.

&

Wills

Note: If you have not made a will yet, you really should consider it!

House Deeds:

Location:

Notes:

Wills:

Name:

Location:

Notes:

Name:

Location:

Notes:

Insurance

This section is really for those insurances that you might forget about, such as life insurance. If you do record house and car insurance here, I suggest you do it in light pencil to allow changes to be made in the future.

Type:

Company:

Renewal date:

Amount:

Type:

Company:

Renewal date:

Amount:

Type:

Company:

Renewal date:

Amount:

Insurance

This section is really for those insurances that you might forget about, such as life insurance. If you do record house and car insurance here, I suggest you do it in light pencil to allow changes to be made in the future.

Type:

Company:

Renewal date:

Amount:

Type:

Company:

Renewal date:

Amount:

Type:

Company:

Renewal date:

Amount:

Insurance

This section is really for those insurances that you might forget about, such as life insurance. If you do record house and car insurance here, I suggest you do it in light pencil to allow changes to be made in the future.

Type:

Company:

Renewal date:

Amount:

Type:

Company:

Renewal date:

Amount:

Type:

Company:

Renewal date:

Amount:

Pensions

This section is to record any private pensions you have had, including the dates you paid into them.

Company:

From: To:

Company:

From: To:

Company:

From: To:

Company:

From: To:

Company:

From: To:

Cars

Car description:

Road tax due:

MOT due:

Service due:

Car description:

Road tax due:

MOT due:

Service due:

Car description:

Road tax due:

MOT due:

Service due:

January
Birthdays

1	2	3	4
5	6	7	8
9	10	11	12
13	14	15	16
17	18	19	20
21	22	23	24
25	26	27	28
29	30	31	

February

Birthdays

1	2	3	4
5	6	7	8
9	10	11	12
13	14	15	16
17	18	19	20
21	22	23	24
25	26	27	28
29			

March
Birthdays

1	2	3	4
5	6	7	8
9	10	11	12
13	14	15	16
17	18	19	20
21	22	23	24
25	26	27	28
29	30	31	

April
Birthdays

1	2	3	4
5	6	7	8
9	10	11	12
13	14	15	16
17	18	19	20
21	22	23	24
25	26	27	28
29	30		

May

Birthdays

1	2	3	4
5	6	7	8
9	10	11	12
13	14	15	16
17	18	19	20
21	22	23	24
25	26	27	28
29	30	31	

June

Birthdays

1	2	3	4
5	6	7	8
9	10	11	12
13	14	15	16
17	18	19	20
21	22	23	24
25	26	27	28
29	30		

July

Birthdays

1	2	3	4
5	6	7	8
9	10	11	12
13	14	15	16
17	18	19	20
21	22	23	24
25	26	27	28
29	30	31	

August

Birthdays

1	2	3	4
5	6	7	8
9	10	11	12
13	14	15	16
17	18	19	20
21	22	23	24
25	26	27	28
29	30	31	

September

Birthdays

1	2	3	4
5	6	7	8
9	10	11	12
13	14	15	16
17	18	19	20
21	22	23	24
25	26	27	28
29	30		

October

Birthdays

1	2	3	4
5	6	7	8
9	10	11	12
13	14	15	16
17	18	19	20
21	22	23	24
25	26	27	28
29	30	31	

November Birthdays

1	2	3	4
5	6	7	8
9	10	11	12
13	14	15	16
17	18	19	20
21	22	23	24
25	26	27	28
29	30		

December

Birthdays

1	2	3	4
5	6	7	8
9	10	11	12
13	14	15	16
17	18	19	20
21	22	23	24
25	26	27	28
29	30	31	

Passwords

Note: For security reasons, it is better to record information here which will help you to recall your passwords rather than actually writing down your passwords. However, if you do decide to write them down, make sure you keep this book in a very safe place.

Website:

Password:

Other security:

Notes:

Website:

Password:

Other security:

Notes:

Website:

Password:

Other security:

Notes:

Passwords

Note: For security reasons, it is better to record information here which will help you to recall your passwords rather than actually writing down your passwords. However, if you do decide to write them down, make sure you keep this book in a very safe place.

Website:

Password:

Other security:

Notes:

Website:

Password:

Other security:

Notes:

Website:

Password:

Other security:

Notes:

Passwords

Note: For security reasons, it is better to record information here which will help you to recall your passwords rather than actually writing down your passwords. However, if you do decide to write them down, make sure you keep this book in a very safe place.

Website:

Password:

Other security:

Notes:

Website:

Password:

Other security:

Notes:

Website:

Password:

Other security:

Notes:

Passwords

Note: For security reasons, it is better to record information here which will help you to recall your passwords rather than actually writing down your passwords. However, if you do decide to write them down, make sure you keep this book in a very safe place.

Website:

Password:

Other security:

Notes:

Website:

Password:

Other security:

Notes:

Website:

Password:

Other security:

Notes:

Passwords

Note: For security reasons, it is better to record information here which will help you to recall your passwords rather than actually writing down your passwords. However, if you do decide to write them down, make sure you keep this book in a very safe place.

Website:

Password:

Other security:

Notes:

Website:

Password:

Other security:

Notes:

Website:

Password:

Other security:

Notes:

Passwords

Note: For security reasons, it is better to record information here which will help you to recall your passwords rather than actually writing down your passwords. However, if you do decide to write them down, make sure you keep this book in a very safe place.

Website:

Password:

Other security:

Notes:

Website:

Password:

Other security:

Notes:

Website:

Password:

Other security:

Notes:

Banking

Note: For security reasons, it is better to record information here which will help you to recall your PIN numbers and passwords rather than actually writing them down. However, if you do decide to write them down, make sure you keep this book in a very safe place, and certainly not with your bank cards.

Bank:

PIN:

Passwords:

Other security:

Notes:

Bank:

PIN:

Passwords:

Other security:

Notes:

Banking

Note: For security reasons, it is better to record information here which will help you to recall your PIN numbers and passwords rather than actually writing them down. However, if you do decide to write them down, make sure you keep this book in a very safe place, and certainly not with your bank cards.

Bank:

PIN:

Passwords:

Other security:

Notes:

Bank:

PIN:

Passwords:

Other security:

Notes:

Banking

Note: For security reasons, it is better to record information here which will help you to recall your PIN numbers and passwords rather than actually writing them down. However, if you do decide to write them down, make sure you keep this book in a very safe place, and certainly not with your bank cards.

Bank:

PIN:

Passwords:

Other security:

Notes:

Bank:

PIN:

Passwords:

Other security:

Notes:

Banking

Note: For security reasons, it is better to record information here which will help you to recall your PIN numbers and passwords rather than actually writing them down. However, if you do decide to write them down, make sure you keep this book in a very safe place, and certainly not with your bank cards.

Bank:

PIN:

Passwords:

Other security:

Notes:

Bank:

PIN:

Passwords:

Other security:

Notes:

Notes

Notes

Notes

Notes

Notes

www.ingramcontent.com/pod-product-compliance
Lightning Source LLC
Chambersburg PA
CBHW081237280526
45787CB00006B/2701